P9-DGB-163

A Pocket Guide to

Hiking

on Mount Desert Island

2nd Edition

This guide is dedicated to the hard-working men and women who share their love of Mount Desert Island with all of us by toiling to maintain and care for the trails and paths on Mount Desert Island. From seasonal trail crews employed by the National Park Service and Friends of Acadia, to volunteers working as groups and individuals, we owe them all our deepest thanks and gratitude.

Copyright © 2012 by Earl D. Brechlin
First edition published 1996

ISBN 978-1-60893-045-6

Cover photograph by Eco Photography

Printed in the United States

5   4   3   2   1

Down East

Distributed to the trade by National Book Network

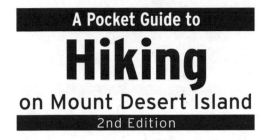

A Pocket Guide to
Hiking
on Mount Desert Island
2nd Edition

BY **EARL D. BRECHLIN**
MAPS BY **RUTH ANN HILL**

Down East

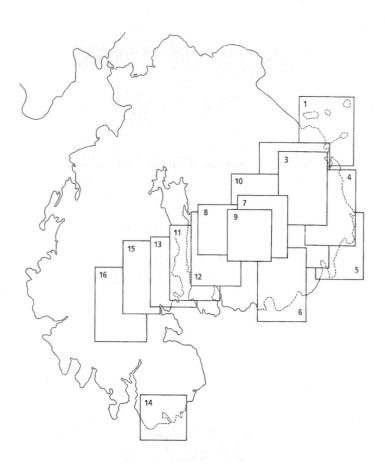

CONTENTS

Introduction

More than one hundred years ago, when the first "Rusticators," inspired by the paintings of Thomas Cole and others of the Hudson River School, discovered Mount Desert Island, hiking, or simply walking as it was called then, was the primary form of recreational and social activity.

Leisurely all-day walks, "tramps" as they were called, with friends and a picnic lunch, with plenty of stops for passionate discussion of the literature and politics of the day, were the rage. There were no auto roads through Acadia National Park, indeed, until 1917 there were no cars allowed on Mount Desert Island. Acadia National Park itself did not exist in National Monument form until 1916, taking the name Acadia in 1929. As the popularity of the island increased, Village Improvement Societies formed in each community. Along with civic improvements such as parks and safer water supplies, they worked with a group called the Hancock County Trustees for Public Reservations and with George B. Dorr, the park's first superintendent, to create the network of hiking trails we enjoy today.

It is said that at the peak, more than 200 miles of maintained hiking trails criss-crossed Acadia's barren summits and ran down the steep-side valleys and along the rocky shore. Each trail is unique in the terrain it traverses, the views it offers, and in the tale it tells of the island's rich geologic, ecologic, and human history. Unlike anywhere else in New England, the trails on MDI provide views quickly as they ascend to open, alpine-like summits. Only here, where climate zones overlap, can so many different types of flora and fauna be found in such proximity.

While not big by the standards of the White Mountains to the west and lofty mile-high Katahdin to the north, the views from Acadia's summits are unsurpassed and offer up dazzling 360-degree panoramas.

Although not all the original miles of trails are still mapped and cared for, hiking, whether along a quiet lake shore, through misty silence of the deep forest, or punctuated by brisk winds on open summits, remains one of the prime recreational activities and one of the best ways to discover the secret beauty and majesty of Mount Desert Island—much as those first visitors did more than a century ago.

Protecting the Resource

With just over 44,000 acres, Acadia is one of the smallest national parks. Much of the activity associated with nearly three million visitors annually is concentrated on the Eastern side of Mount Desert Island. Because of this intensive use visitors must take it upon themselves to be wise stewards of the area's natural beauty.

Pack it in, pack it out—Take nothing but photographs and leave nothing but footprints. If you find litter on the trail, please pick it up and pack it out.

Stay on the trail—Especially on high open ridges, the sub-alpine vegetation is extremely sensitive to damage by walkers. Stay on the trail and on bare rock whenever possible. In muddy areas, stay on the rough log "bog walks." Resist the urge to skirt muddy areas as that only widens the trail and does unnecessary damage.

Preserve vegetation—Don't break branches or trample plants unnecessarily. While picking of wild blueberries and other fruits for personal consumption is allowed, taking mushrooms and other plants is not.

Leave wildlife alone—Observing an animal in the wild is one of the real thrills of hiking. Don't harass the animals or offer them food. Once animals are imprinted with the notion of people as a source of food, they can drop their natural fear of humans. This can cause them great harm later and can also affect their abilities to rely on natural food sources.

Pets—All pets in Acadia National Park must remain on leashes. Owners can be summonsed for unleashed pets.

Fire—Fires are allowed only in designated campgrounds and picnic areas.

Camping—Camping is allowed only in the Blackwoods Campground and the Seawall Campground in the park and in private campgrounds nearby. Rangers conduct regular backcountry patrols and from time to time even use night vision equipment to catch scofflaws.

Swimming—Many of the larger lakes on Mount Desert Island are public water supplies for area towns. Eagle Lake, Bubble Pond, Jordan Pond, Upper and Lower Hadlock Pond, and portions of Long Pond in Southwest Harbor are all restricted to swimming, wading, or allowing pets to make contact with the water.

User rules—Bicycles and horses are banned from all hiking trails. Some restrictions apply concerning horse and bicycle use on the carriage road system. For example, horses are not allowed on the carriage road around Witch Hole Pond or on the west side of Eagle Lake. Bicycles are banned on the Rockefeller-owned carriage roads in Seal Harbor. When in doubt, check with park officials. Carriage Road courtesy rules call for bicyclists to yield to walkers and horses and for hikers to yield to horses.

Private Property—Throughout the park are "inholdings," areas of private property surrounding by government land. Some parts of the island, such as the land and paths around Little Long Pond in Seal Harbor, are private property yet abut the park and are open to the public. Also, many areas, such as the Shore Path in Bar Harbor, are also privately owned. Always respect private property rights and never trespass.

Respect Solitude—One of the hardest things to achieve in our modern world is solitude. While no one can lay claim to any part of the park as theirs, respect people's privacy in the wild. Don't crowd other visitors. Don't hog the area around summit so others too can savor the moment of reaching the top. Don't throw rocks off cliffs as others may be hiking below.

YOU CAN HELP

The non-profit group Friends of Acadia, in cooperation with the National Park Service, sponsors regular trail maintenance work on a regular schedule all summer. Check local publications for dates and times. Contact FOA at 207-288-3340 or Acadia National Park at 207-288-3338 for information.

Be sure to read the following sections. They will help make your hike on Mount Desert Island more safe and enjoyable.

Heading Out

Proper preparation for a day in the wild means being prepared for any eventuality. With so many to choose from, it is easy to select a route for your individual fitness level and the abilities of those in your party. Take it slow. There is plenty of time. If you set out to "just do it," you are missing the point and won't get to savor much of what Acadia has to offer.

As Mark Twain once said of all weather in New England "if you don't like it, wait a minute, it'll change." That goes double for Mount Desert Island, where not only does the weather change several times in a day, but also where weather conditions can vary greatly depending on one's proximity to the ocean and change in altitude. It is not unusual for it to be sunny in Bar Harbor while it is raining at Jordan Pond and Ocean Drive is socked-in with pea soup fog.

Daylight fades quickly in autumn, so make sure you have plenty of time to complete your walk before dark. It doesn't hurt to put a headlamp or small flashlight in your daypack along with other essentials.

Studies have shown that the average temperature drops a degree or two for each three to four hundred foot elevation gain. Add in a steady wind and most summits are markedly cooler than the surrounding lowlands.

CLOTHING

Even on the hottest days be sure to pack a wind and waterproof jacket. A hiker soaked in a passing shower and then buffeted by high winds can succumb to hypothermia, the sometimes deadly lowering of the body's core temperature, even when the mercury is above 60 degrees. A good percentage of body heat is lost through the head. Packing a hat is also a good idea. A disposable "space blanket" is also a popular pack item.

Proper footwear is vital. Many trails traverse slippery ledges that become treacherous after a rain. In some areas the dark algae that flourish in the runoff after rains is particularly slippery. A good, solid, hard-soled boot that also provides ankle support is vital. Sneakers or sports sandals offer little protection to the bottoms of feet while leaping from boulder to boulder on some trails. Sections of trails with iron ladder rungs on cliff faces are also difficult in flexible footwear.

To help prevent blisters, wear a polypropylene undersock

under a heavy boot sock. The inner sock will help wick moisture away from your feet while the outer layer will reduce abrasion. A small piece of moleskin foam tucked into your first aid kit is invaluable to covering hot spots before they develop into blisters.

WATER

Acadia is graced with scores of brooks and numerous large lakes. And, one of the real treats of hiking through the backcountry is a refreshing drink from a mountain stream. Still, bring some water with you on a hike. Even the most reliable mountain springs can go dry in high summer. Few pollutants threaten the pristine quality of Mount Desert Island's water, although some evidence of the giardia, a naturally occurring parasite that can cause serious intestinal problems known as "Beaver Fever," has been detected. The chance of you contracting this problem, even when drinking unfiltered water, is small, but officials advise filtering or treating water before consumption. If the choice is between a powerful thirst and an unfiltered, yet clear-running source, by all means drink.

Alcoholic beverages and most sodas only seem to quench your thirst, but actually act as diruetics. They end up increasing your body's need for water.

FINDING THE TRAIL

Most trails in Acadia National Park are clearly marked on the ground and show up well on the many maps that are available.

Trail heads in Acadia are marked with lettered signs carved into wooden posts. Blue paint blazes on bare ledge, stone cairns, and vestiges of old metal markers fastened to trees help lead the way when the worn footpath or evidence of brush cutting is less apparent. Do not damage cairns or construct new ones.

Trail intersections are marked with carved wooden signs on posts giving directions and distances. Occasionally, some signs may be missing, so follow the map carefully as you walk.

If you lose the trail, return to the last obvious marker and have a member of your party fan out to find the next one before proceeding. This is especially important on the steeper trails, such as the Precipice, where switchbacks are plentiful. So many people take wrong turns at some spots that it creates false trails that quickly fade or stop abruptly. Piles of logs or rocks are often used by trail crews to block passage on false or closed trails. Hikers sometimes spot the remains of abandoned paths called "ghost trails." Be careful not to be confused by these or by illegal trails created by "trail phantoms." If you notice a fresh, unmapped trail, or trail workers not sporting uniforms or clothing or hats identifying them as volunteers, notify rangers immediately.

If you do become disoriented, remember that, in general, most ridgelines on MDI run in a north-south direction. Most ridges have trails that can easily be followed to safety. "Bushwacking" off the trail, particularly in an east or west direction, can be hazardous. Even a map with 50-foot contour lines does not show a lot of deadly 40-foot drops!

Stick together, or at least make arrangements to regroup members of your party at major intersections or summits, and take a head count before proceeding.

Scores of people become separated from their group or are reported overdue in Acadia each year. Most are quickly located by park rangers or members of the volunteer Mount Desert Island Search and Rescue Group.

If hiking alone, be sure to leave a note detailing your route and the time of your expected return. That way, should you have a problem on the trail, someone will be able to summon assistance.

If darkness falls and you have not found your way, stay put, help will come. Most of the serious injuries from falls involving lost hikers in Acadia have occurred after dark. Cell phones are allowed in the park and work well from most summits and ridges. In an emergency call 911.

OTHER CONCERNS

Insects—Especially during late May and early June, bitting blackflies can make any walk in the forest a miserable experience. On any damp day without a breeze, mosquitos can also be a problem, particularly in heavily vegetated areas. Later in the season, moose and deer flies may be bothersome.

Commercial repellents containing DEET seem to work best, although formulas containing the highest percentage of the chemical can damage plastic surfaces if it comes off your skin onto cameras and binoculars. Natural repellents are also available, as are brands especially formulated for children.

Snakes—There are no poisonous snakes on Mount Desert Island.

Coyotes—Coyotes are plentiful in Acadia and can often be heard calling or running in packs at night. There is no record of them ever attacking a human here.

Sunburn—Forgetting to use sun block while hiking or basking in the sun along the shore has ruined more vacations that any other affliction. Use of a lotion with at least an SPF # of 30 or higher is crucial.

Fire—In 1947 a devastating forest fire swept across Mount Desert Island, burning thousands of acres and destroying more than 100 homes. When fire dangers rise, traditionally in late summer and early fall, park officials will sometimes ban smoking on the trails.

Lyme Disease—Some ticks found on Mount Desert Island have evidence of debilitating Lyme disease, so general tick precautions are in order. Avoid brushy and grassy areas and check yourself carefully for ticks after each excursion. Ticks do not attach themselves immediately, so early detection is important. If you find a tick, follow standard first aid recommendations for removal.

An infected bite often produces a red rash, often in a ring around it. Symptoms, including heart, breathing, and arthritis-like difficulties, may not appear until much later. Early detection makes treatment easy. In later stages, Lyme disease is difficult to treat. If in doubt, contact a physician.

Overview

The hikes profiled in this book are arranged geographically. All the hikes in a given chapter appear on the chapter map. The sketch map accompanying the table of contents indicates the area shown in each map. On pages 22 and 23 is a map of the entire island and a key to the symbols used in the hiking route maps.

Notice that suggested times have not been included. Every hiker is different, with those in great shape being able to make several miles per hour in mountainous terrain, while those who prefer a slower pace may only make a mile per hour. Review any planned trip with your condition, the weather, the length of the trail and elevation gain, and difficulty all in mind. When in doubt, leave yourself extra time. Check the weather forecast before leaving.

The following difficulty ratings for Acadia's trails closely follow those established by the National Park Service:

Easy—Fairly level ground, small up and down hill sections, good footing.

Moderate—Uneven ground, some steep uphills with loose rock or soil. Attention to foot placement necessary.

Strenuous—Steady climbs and descents. Long uphill stretches with careful attention needed to foot placement. Some use of hands.

Ladder—Iron rungs or handrails on some sections. Steep dropoffs. Necessary use of hands. Very difficult.

CONNECTOR TRAILS

In recent years, Friends of Acadia, private landowners, and the park have worked together to create new trails connecting villages with the park. They include the Great Meadow Loop

(Easy), and the Schooner Head Path (Easy) in Bar Harbor and the Duck Brook Connector (Easy) on Eden Street in Bar Harbor. Use them whenever possible.

Acadia Access

ENTRANCE FEES

Acadia National Park is a fee area. Although there is just one fee collection booth on the Park Loop Road, visitors are encouraged to pick up an entrance pass at locations throughout the park and in town. Passes are available for various time periods. Each November and December, annual passes, which include window stickers for two vehicles, go on sale for half price.

Part of the fees collected go to cover general park operations and also to support the Island Explorer. Both park campgrounds charge fees.

TAKE THE BUS

The Island Explorer is a free shuttle bus system that runs throughout the park and between various area towns. It is funded with entrance fees, government subsidies, and donations from corporations such as L.L. Bean, Friends of Acadia, and area communities.

The hub of the bus system is the Bar Harbor Village Green, where most routes intersect. Routes regularly stop at all campgrounds and hotels. Drivers will pull over if flagged down anywhere it is safe to stop.

The bus makes it possible for hikers to do point-to-point routes through Acadia without needing any car, much less two. The buses can carry bikes and there is even a special shuttle van with trailer that provides multiple trips daily between the Village Green and the north end of Eagle Lake, where several popular carrige roads are located.

Plans call for the Island Explorer to work from a new hub and visitor center at Crippen Creek in Trenton, where day-use visitors can leave their vehicles.

WINTER ACCESS

In winter, the park visitor center shifts operations to headquarters on Route 233.

Trailheads can be accessed from state roads that are plowed in the winter. Hiking is not restricted, although many steeper trails are too dangerous except for those with technical gear.

One lane of the park's Ocean Drive is kept plowed with access via the Schooner Head Road from Bar Harbor. The unplowed loop, including the Cadillac Mountain Summit Road, is open for hikers, snowshoers, cross-country skiers, and snowmobilers. With a few exceptions, no motorized use, such as snowmobiles, is allowed on the 45 miles of carriage roads. All dogs must be kept on a leash shorter than six feet.

The Blackwoods Campground is officially closed, but walk-in users with a permit can stay at a limited number of sites.

Volunteer cross-country-ski groomers from the Acadia Winter Trails Association, an arm of Friends of Acadia, do their best to keep 32 miles of carriage roads in top shape. Please don't walk or allow pets to damage the track. For the latest ski information visit:

nps.gov/acad/planyourvisit/crosscountryskiing.htm

Mount Desert Island

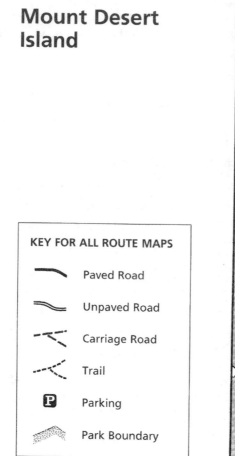

KEY FOR ALL ROUTE MAPS

⌇	Paved Road
⌇	Unpaved Road
⌇	Carriage Road
⌇	Trail
🅿	Parking
⌇	Park Boundary

Legend

⌇	PAVED ROAD
⌇	UNPAVED ROAD
LR	PARK LOOP ROAD
⌇	NATIONAL PARK

Western Bay

Bartlett
Island

Long
Pond

Hardwood
Island

Seal
Cove
Pond

Blue Hill
Bay

102

0   1 MILE

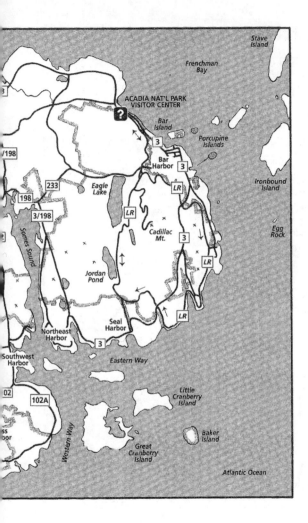

MAP 1: BAR HARBOR VILLAGE

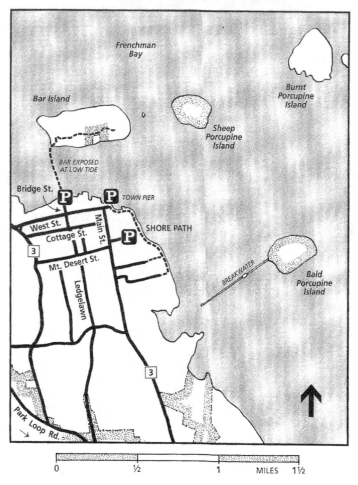

1

Bar Harbor Village

BAR HARBOR SHORE PATH (EASY)

For more than 100 years the Shore Path in Bar Harbor has attracted strollers with its ocean views and cool breezes. Maintained by the Village Improvement Association, it is located on private land open to the public through the graciousness of the owners. Please remember this and respect their privacy.

The path begins on the east side of the municipal pier, curves along the town beach and past the Bar Harbor Inn. The main building here, which houses the Reading Room Restaurant and Gatsby's Terrace, was built during Prohibition as a "Reading Room" for wealthy summer residents to enjoy a discrete libation.

Just past the inn property the path skirts the shore along Grant's Park, also known as Albert's Meadow. The park is open dawn to dusk and is an excellent spot for a picnic or just a place to sit and watch the comings and goings when one of the more than 100 ocean-going cruise ships like Cunard's *Queen Elizabeth* that visit Frenchman Bay each year is anchored nearby.

The remainder of the ¾-mile path remains much as it was long ago as it skirts the front of some of the remaining mansions from the town's Golden Age. Several have been converted into cozy inns.

As you walk, imagine the summer family that owned the Hope diamond, their house on the water now gone. Local residents remember it was not uncommon for their children to play with the priceless jewel, now housed in the Smithsonian in Washington, D.C., on the front lawn!

During the day, lobstermen and their boats can be seen working just offshore. Seabirds can be seen, and occasionally porpoises and minke whales can be spotted frolicking in the bay.

Off to the southeast lies the Bar Harbor Breakwater, built by the U.S. Army Corps of Engineers in 1901. Never completed, it is 100 feet wide at its base and rises 60 feet from the ocean bottom.

A connecting path turns right off the Shore Path and connects with Hancock Street for a quick return to town. A little farther, the Shore Path ends with a right turn up a path that ends on Wayman Lane. A right turn at the end of either of these streets will return down Main Street to the downtown.

BAR ISLAND (EASY)

Connected to the village at low tide by a wide gravel and mud bar covered in places by mussel beds, Bar Island is an oasis of quietitude just a few hundred yards from one of the busiest tourist destinations on the East Coast.

Because of the area's sweeping tides (which average 12 feet), Bar Island is only accessible two times daily. Depending on conditions, the bar emerges about two hours after high tide and remains uncovered for two to three hours. **Watch the tide and the time carefully!** Trying to cross while the tide is coming in is very dangerous. If you miss the tide you will have a long wait. Consult local tide tables before going on this walk. Although motorists sometimes drive out onto the bar, resist parking there as several unattended cars a year are submerged by the incoming water. There are places to park on the northern end of Bridge Street where the bar begins.

There are not too many places where you can literally stroll along the ocean bottom. Once up off the rock-strewn shore of Bar Island, the character of this hardwood forested island changes. There is a large field in the island's interior and an unofficial trail to the tall, treeless knob on the eastern end. There are spectacular views of the village of Bar Harbor and the mountains beyond from the top.

At one time, Bar Island was home to several families who had farms, gardens, boat-building shops, and fish weirs.

2

Cadillac Mountain

At 1,530 feet high, Cadillac Mountain is the highest point within 50 miles of the coast from Maine to Rio de Janeiro in Brazil.

Although it is not the first place in the United States touched by the sun's rays each morning, visitors on the summit may be the first people to see the sun dawn over America on a new day. Watching the sunrise and the sunset are popular activities. While access by motor road is possible now, years ago the only way up Cadillac was by foot. For a time, the Green Mountain Railway Company operated a steam-driven cog railway up the mountain's west side. Passengers took a buggy ride from Bar Harbor to a steam launch docked at the north end of Eagle Lake. The boat brought them to the railway terminus on the east shore of the lake. The trip by cog railway was so slow that passengers actually had time to jump off and pick blueberries along the way!

After a few years the line went bust and the tracks were removed. The locomotive and cars are now owned by the cog railway line up Mount Washington in New Hampshire.

MAP 2: CADILLAC MOUNTAIN

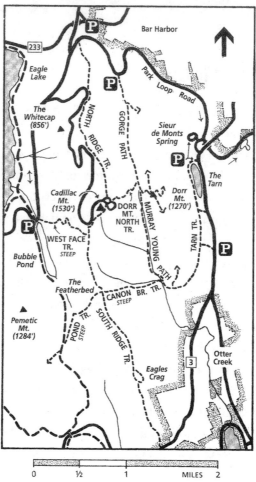

Over the years, several hotels were built and were either torn down or burned down. The park service has rest rooms and a concession shop on the summit.

While a trip to the top of the Mount Desert Island's tallest mountain is high on many hikers' lists, some find it anti-climactic, when, after a long, hard climb, they encounter the throngs of tourists, buses, and recreational vehicles that crowd the summit on a typical day in season. Still, the walk is worth every effort.

There are few places where such stunning views unfold for 360 degrees. To the south lies the unbroken expanse of the Atlantic. Look closely and you'll swear you can see the curvature of the earth! That small smudge to the south with the flashing light is Mount Desert Rock, more than 25 miles offshore. Now automated, it is used as a research station by College of the Atlantic.

To the east, the Down East coast continues to Canada. In the west, the lesser peaks of Mount Desert Island lie in a row. In the distance look for Blue Hill and the Camden Hills.

To the north lie the hills of Lurcerne, nearly 40 miles off. When the sun is low in the morning, look closely on the horizon where the hills dip down. The gray silhouette behind is none other than mile-high Katahdin, the highest peak in Maine and the northern terminus of the Appalachian Trail. As the crow flies, Katahdin lies 150 miles away. That's excellent visibility in anyone's book.

While there is a well-developed path and patio near the parking area that people believe is the summit, the high point on Cadillac Mountain is actually out behind the gift shop, where the radio antenna is located. Follow the gravel road to the spot and look for the three-inch U.S. Geological Survey medal cemented to a ledge to visit the true summit. Because of the large number of possible loop trips, as well as out and back excursions involving Cadillac Mountain trails, each one is described individually. Mix and match to suit individual taste.

NORTH RIDGE TRAIL (STRENUOUS)

This hike begins on the Park Loop Road across from an overlook that frames views of Bar Harbor and Frenchman Bay.

The trail rises steadily toward the summit, at times skirting the motor road to the top. After leaving the road for the last time about 1.5 miles from the start, the trail passes near a carving in a ledge that legend has it is a Maltese Cross left by Explorer Samuel de Champlain's crew in 1604. Only a thin iron post betrays its location today.

The trail alternates between sections of scrub pines and open ledges on the just-under-two-mile long trip.

SOUTH RIDGE TRAIL (STRENUOUS)

One of the longest trails on Mount Desert Island, the South Ridge Trail up Cadillac is also one of the most popular. A feeder trail connects it directly with the nearby Blackwoods Campground.

Most people start at Route 3 in Otter Creek, just west of the entrance to the campground. The trail ascends gradually for .75 mile before rising sharply onto Eagle's Crag. A small loop trail heads right and the views to the east make it worth the effort. If you take the left path you will soon begin the long walk along the mountain's backbone. Take note as you leave the mixed woods and enter the world of bare ledge and jack pines. The vegetation change marks the line where the Great Forest Fire of 1947 was stopped.

The trail continues the gradual rise cresting over open ledge before descending slightly to a depression pond called The Featherbed at 1.75 miles. Occasionally beavers live here, but the pond often dries up.

Trail crews have build rustic benches here so it is a good rest stop.

At an intersection, the Canon Brook Trail enters from the east and the west.

Climbing sharply now, the trail continues north, leaving most major vegetation behind. Winds here usually blow strong. At two miles the West Face Trail enters from the left. You will really notice the elevation gain now. Views abound in every direction.

After skirting the auto road, the trail heads more northeasterly before arriving at the summit in a total of 3.5 miles.

When planning a trip, the South Ridge Trail is the best for descent as it is easy on the knees and the best views are ahead of you.

WEST FACE TRAIL (STRENUOUS)

A hike up the West Face trail is one of the quickest ways to gain altitude on Cadillac. It is a very steep trail, however, and has several sections on very steep, smooth granite ledges that make for tricky footing. It is a very difficult trail to descend. Some hikers say it's like the famed Precipice, without ladder rungs.

Begin at the Bubble Pond Parking Area and walk to the north end of the lake. The trail begins to the left after crossing the outlet stream on a small bridge. Almost immediately the trail begins zigzaging up a series of steep ledges adorned with cedar and pine. There are excellent places to stop and enjoy views to the west and of the pond below.

After several steep pitches, the terrain opens up and the trail joins the South Ridge Trail at 0.85 mile.

CANON BROOK TRAIL–WEST (STRENUOUS)

From the Featherbed, the Canon Brook Trail goes both east and west. To the west, it skirts the north end of the wet ground, traversing smooth ledges in deep woods and then drops literally like a rock off the west side of the mountain. Improvements by trail crews have added stone steps and some handrailings to sections of loose dirt and rock that previously could only be traversed in a style that could be politely termed a "controlled crash."

Bog walk planks, foot bridges, and stonework complete this renovation. The trail levels off after 0.25 mile bottoms out in the marshy area between Cadillac and Pemetic before heading southwest to join with the Bubble and Jordan Pond Path, a carriage road, at 1.5 miles.

CANON BROOK TRAIL–EAST (STRENUOUS)

The name Canon Brook is a classical mapmaker's mistake. Originally called Canyon Brook, the "y" was dropped in later map editions and copies. Canyon makes more sense because the trail follows a steep, rocky stream-bed chasm on the east face. From the Featherbed, the trail hops, skips, and jumps on rocks down a muddy stream bed heading east. After just over 0.5 mile the trail turns hard right and begins following Canon Brook in earnest. Shortly, the trail emerges on ledges swept clean by spring torrents. Footing is tricky on the steep smooth rock and trail markers are sometimes hard to follow.

At 0.65 mile the trail overlooks the actual canyon, which is about ten feet wide and 15 feet deep. Continue carefully down the right side of the chasm to boulders that offer steps down on overgrown talus slopes. Go right where the trail joins up with the A. Murray Young Path at a distance of 0.8 mile.

The Canon Brook Trail continues over the bottom of Dorr and eventually turns into the Kane Path along the Tarn.

A. MURRAY YOUNG PATH (STRENUOUS)

Reached from Route 3 via the Kane Path and the Canon Brook Trail, the A. Murray Young Path offers one of the most interesting ways up Cadillac. Just after passing the Canon Brook Turnoff at 0.75, this trail begins working its way up the brook that drains the valley between Cadillac and Dorr. Soon you pass a massive boulder in mid-stream with a memorial plaque to Young placed there by the Village Improvement Association.

The trail begins ascending more steeply, at places clinging to the west side of the gorge.

At 0.5 mile after the Canon Brook intersection, the trail enters a broad valley that once held a beaver pond. The trail is narrow. Watch for those dreaded "leaves of three" very carefully as poison ivy grows here.

After a steep, rocky section at the head of the valley, the trail levels off over rocky ground and joins the Gorge Trail between Cadillac and Dorr. The A. Murray Young Path turns right to the top of Dorr. Turn left and climb steeply on the last stretch of the Gorge Path for 0.5 mile.

THE GORGE PATH (STRENUOUS)

The Gorge Path is one of the fastest and, in summer coolest, ways to climb Cadillac.

Begin on the Park Loop Road at the pull-off and trail head adjacent to the bridge spanning Kebo Brook between Kebo Mountain and Cadillac.

The trail drops immediately to the cool, tree-lined shade beneath the bridge. It then follows the brook uphill before meeting with the intersection of the Hemlock Trail in 0.5 mile. Shortly, the path gets much steeper as it crisscrosses the brook over large mossy boulders. Even in high summer there is likely to be some water in pools and clefts along this route. There are no views to speak of, although the real beauty of this path is in the forest details and weathered rocks.

After just under a mile of steady climbing, the trail emerges from the dark forest into the cleft between Cadillac and Dorr Mountains. Turn right for another 0.5 mile of steep climbing over open ledges to the summit.

Dorr and Kebo Mountains

DORR MOUNTAIN (STRENUOUS)

There is only one way to describe the trails on Dorr Mountain—vertical.

Whether it is the Ladder Trail with, according to trail historian Tom St. Germain, exactly 1005 stone steps, or the other east-face options, there is little level going until you are well on your way to the top of this 1270-foot edifice.

LADDER TRAIL (LADDER)

At one time the Ladder Trail was the main access to the top and it is a good place to start. Begin on Route 3 near the wooden trailhead post, just south of the Tarn. A short downhill stretch brings you to an intersection with the Kane Path and Canon Brook Trail. Signs will point you to the base of the Ladder Trail.

MAP 3: DORR & KEBO MTNS.

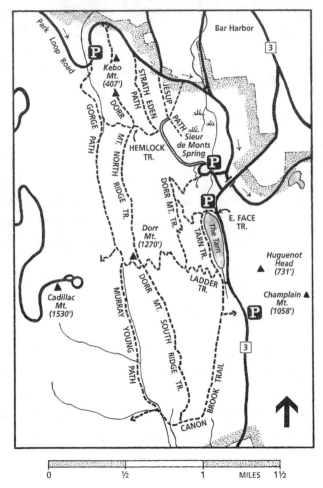

Bar Harbor

3

Park Loop Road

P

Kebo Mt. (407')

STRATH EDEN PATH

JESUP PATH

Sieur de Monts Spring

GORGE PATH

MT. NORTH RIDGE TR.

DORR

HEMLOCK TR.

DORR MT. TR.

P

P

E. FACE TR.

The Tarn

TARN TR.

Dorr Mt. (1270')

Cadillac Mt. (1530')

Huguenot Head (731')

LADDER TR.

Champlain Mt. (1058')

MURRAY YOUNG PATH

DORR MT. SOUTH RIDGE TR.

P

3

CANON

BROOK TRAIL

0   ½   1   MILES   1½

Almost immediately, steep stone steps ascend up the side of the mountain along an angled fault in the granite. The rise is steady, almost unforgiving, for 0.5 mile, but views come quickly. A couple hand railings and ladder rungs assist you along the way. There are no sources of water and in summer the sun mercilessly bakes the rock.

Just as the trail levels out, it meets with the Schiff Path. Bear left for the meandering yet steady trip to the relatively small and rock-strewn summit for a total hike of just under a mile.

Views include the activity on Cadillac Mountain to the west and nice angles on Bar Harbor and Frenchman Bay to the north and the ocean to the south.

Return by retracing your steps down the Schiff Path and enjoy the switchbacks. It connects to three options for descent, including Kurt Diederich's Climb that ends at the north end of the Tarn.

The other options on that face accessed by the Schiff Path include the Emery Path and the Homan's Path. Both return to the general area of the spring. The Homan's Path was closed for a time after an earthquake in 2006 dropped a large boulder across it.

Another option is to take the more gradual South Ridge Trail down 1.2 miles and turn left on the comparatively flat

Canon Brook Trail, which loops back to the north and connects with the Kane Path along the Tarn for a longer loop of 3.0 miles.

KEBO MOUNTAIN (MODERATE)

With three small summits and numerous vegetative zones, Kebo Mountain is a great short hike.

Begin on the Park Loop Road at the Stratheden Path pullout. The path is fairly level as it heads south along the mountain's eastern flank. Several old roads branch off the right and end at small, abandoned quarry sites. The trail then drops steadily to where it meets the Hemlock Trail between Kebo and Dorr Mountains. Turn right and begin a steady ascent.

At the next intersection turn right again and climb the first of Kebo's knobs, which recent GPS data indicate may be the true summit. The trail drops steeply and heads north, gradually climbing the second hump. Open ledges provide wonderful views of Cadillac to the west and Great Meadow Marsh and Bar Harbor to the east. Descend again and pass through interesting groves of trees. Watch out for a sharp right turn. Climb the final peak through a grove of jack pine. The official summit at 407 feet is just ahead. Below you can see portions of the Kebo Valley Golf Course, the ninth oldest in North America.

Continue north and descend steeply. A very slippery and steep section at the end will undoubtedly be a challenge. Turn right after hitting the road for the short jaunt back to the start, for a total distance of just over 1.5 miles.

JESUP TRAIL (EASY)

The wheelchair accessible Jesup Trail begins at Sieur de Monts Spring and heads north through an attractive grove of white birches. Most of the way to the old Hemock Road is on a raised boardwalk with places to sit and birdwatch. Turn left to return (for a walk of 0.5 mile total) or continue north (over non-wheelchair terrain) and hike through the marsh, ending at the Park Loop Road. Turn right and walk a short ways back to the north end of Hemlock Road to return.

MAP 4: CHAMPLAIN MTN

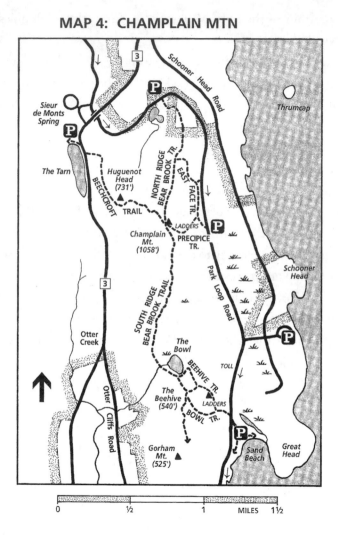

Schooner Head Road

Thrumcap

Sieur de Monts Spring

The Tarn

BEECHCROFT TRAIL

Huguenot Head (731')

NORTH RIDGE BEAR BROOK TR.

EAST FACE TR.

LADDERS

Champlain Mt. (1058')

PRECIPICE TR.

Schooner Head

SOUTH RIDGE BEAR BROOK TRAIL

Park Loop Road

Otter Creek

The Bowl

BEEHIVE TR.

TOLL

The Beehive (540')

LADDERS

BOWL TR.

Otter Cliffs Road

Gorham Mt. (525')

Sand Beach

Great Head

0 ½ 1 MILES 1½

4

Champlain Mountain Area

CHAMPLAIN MOUNTAIN

One of the most popular mountains in the park, 1058-foot-tall Champlain is home to the most rugged and dangerous trails on the East Coast—the Precipice.

There are several ways up, and perhaps more importantly, down, Champlain. Its wide-open summit has spectacular views in all directions. It is the best place to sit and watch all the comings and goings in Frenchman Bay to the east.

Whale-watch, lobster, excursion, and pleasure boats race to and fro among the Porcupine Islands, named years ago for their distinctive shapes.

The red flashing light of Egg Rock Light, now automated, helps guide the more than 100 cruise ships that visit Bar Harbor each year.

THE PRECIPICE (LADDER)

A sign at the trail head in the parking lot on the Park Loop Road warns that the Precipice is not so much a hiking trail as it is a non-techincal climbing route. This cannot be overstated.

Although fatalities are rare and are usually confined to those who wandered off the trail or had an accident while technical climbing, scores of people each year misjudge their abilities and need assistance to get down. **Warning:** *Do not attempt this trail if you have a fear of heights, are not properly dressed, lack proper footwear, or are not physically prepared. Do not leave late in the day when there will not be adequate light to complete your hike. Also, this trail has no water, ever. Hikers can be exposed to the sun, wind, or rain for extended periods. Even relatively level sections can be slippery and hazardous when wet.*

Begin on the steps that lead west from the parking area. The trail runs over ledge and boulders for a few hundred yards to the first ladder rung and handrail at the base of a cliff. The "step" up is five-feet. Rangers like to call this spot "The Eliminator," because people who have trouble here usually have the good sense to turn back.

After the first rung, the trail rises sharply as it heads north to the base of a large boulder field. The climb is steep here, often requiring hands as you follow trail markers over and under truck-size rocks.

The cliffs overlooking the boulder field are home to endangered peregrine falcons, which were reintroduced to the park some years back. Each year a pair returns to raise their chicks on a lofty ledge called a scrape. Until the birds are fledged, the Precipice is closed to make sure human activity doesn't hurt nesting efforts. The closure typically starts in May and lasts until late August. Those who fail to heed closed area signs can be summonsed to court.

Leaving the boulder field behind, the trail continues passing over a wooden footbridge with the aid of extensive iron hand rails. Switchbacks continue north, then south, as more altitude is gained.

The trail turns sharply to the left where a path connecting to the Orange and Black Path (formerly the East Face Trail) enters from the right.

Hands are needed to boost yourself up five- and six-foot-high steps as the trail continues.

Watch to avoid false trails at major turns.

The upper third of the Precipice consists of several switchbacks connected by a series of iron bars pounded into the cliff face as ladder rungs. Several crude iron ladders are also attached as climbing aids.

In some areas, iron bars act as guardrails to catch feet that may slip on narrow ledges. Some handrails are provided. Since dropoffs of several hundred feet are common, watch your step carefully. Try to keep three points of contact with the rock (i.e., two hands and a foot or two feet and a hand, etc.) at all times.

Just as the trail seems to curve left and disappear at the top of a huge drop, you enter a cleft and are back on terra firma.

The trail continues, steeply at times, up the open jack pine woods and over ledges to the summit, for a total trip of just over 1.0 mile.

Rather than descend via the Precipice, which is harder than climbing up and can cause climber jams on busy days, consider taking the North Ridge Trail down.

The Beechcroft Path, which traverses Huguenot Head on its way to the summit of Champlain, branches off just a little to the north. It is very steep and has treacherous footing in spots.

You can also access the Precipice parking area by taking the Schooner Head Path out of Bar Harbor toward Sand Beach and taking a right on Murphy Lane.

NORTH RIDGE TRAIL (STRENUOUS)

From the summit, the North Ridge or Bear Brook Trail heads north over open ledges and through small groves of stunted trees. Watch carefully near the top because misguided hikers insist on building scores of small cairns that can make staying on the true trail difficult.

Along the entire way there will be great views of Bar Harbor and the reknowned genetic research facility The Jackson Laboratory to the north.

About half way keep your eyes out for a circular bronze survey marker with the initials "JDR." It is one of the original makers used by crews working for John D. Rockefeller Jr. as he helped to assemble land to create Acadia National Park.

About 0.5 mile from the summit, turn right on the Orange and Black Path. Descend steeply to a curved path paved with flat granite boulders. A right turn will connect you over a difficult trail to the lower Precipice. A left turn will take you to the Park Loop Road over smooth ledges. A right turn at the road leaves you only a 0.5 mile walk back to your vehicle.

Total distance for the circuit is 2.25 miles.

Staying on the North Ridge section of the Bear Brook Trail brings you quickly to the parking area on the Loop Road at the north end of the mountain. This is a good route to climb and return if the weather is in question.

SOUTH RIDGE TRAIL (STRENUOUS)

The South Ridge portion of the Bear Brook Trail leaves the summit and gradually descends toward the Beehive and the Bowl. The route offers fine views of the ocean and areas to the east and west. Crossing the outlet stream for the Bowl, the trail skirts this high mountain pond. Turn right on the Bowl Trail at the intersection to quickly descend to the Park Loop Road near Sand Beach. The north end of the Bear Brook Trail is a 1.5-mile backtrack along the Park Loop Road.

HUGUENOT HEAD (STRENUOUS)

Built by craftsmen nearly one hundred years ago, the Beachcroft Path up Huguenot Head is one of the most handsome on the island. Its 1,500 winding stone steps and easy grades are so reminiscent of a hobbit road that one almost expects to see Frodo himself strutting down the mountain.

Park in the paved area on the west side of Route 3 just south of the park's Sieur de Monts entrance. The trail starts at the wooden marker and stone steps directly across the road. Maintaining a gradual incline, the path works up the western side of a small hill and then crosses over onto the steep side of the head itself. Here numerous switchbacks help hikers gain altitude quickly. Especially in summer, the sun bakes these ledges and there is no water. Be sure to carry some.

After about 0.5 mile, the trail skirts the actual 731-foot summit (which can be reached by a quick and easy bushwack) and drops down to a small seasonal pond before rising steeply to the summit on Champlain Mountain.

Deer tracks are often seen in the mud around the pond.

Just before descending toward the pond, there are fine open ledges that offer splendid views of the ocean to the south and Dorr and Cadillac Mountains to the west. Below lies the Tarn, a small shallow pond created by a dam built by George B. Dorr, one of the fathers of the park and its first superintendent.

THE BEEHIVE (LADDER)

For a short hike that is long on challenge and reward, yet short on distance and elevation gain, the aptly named, 520-foot-tall Beehive is a good choice.

The trail begins just north of the entrance to the Sand Beach

Parking Area and rises gradually over stepping stones. After a short distance the incline increases and several sloped ledges are crossed. The Ladder Trail goes right at the first intersection, just under 0.25 mile from the start. It quickly begins a series of switchbacks up the face of the beehive. Views of Sand Beach, Great Head, and the entire Ocean Drive start immediately and just keep getting better.

In several places, narrow footbridges have been installed, including a unique one composed of iron bars set horizontally. Hands are definitely needed, and foot and handrails are occasionally provided.

One last steep section is passed before reaching the top at 0.5 mile.

To return, continue north on the Beehive Trail. You can take a shortcut by turning left at the first intersection and descend steeply over boulder fields. A left turn at the next intersection will take you back towards Sand Beach. Or, continue on to the Bowl, a high, nearly round pond hidden behind the Beehive. Stop for a minute to soak your tired feet before skirting the south end of the pond to the next trail intersection. Turn left, rise briefly, and then descend steadily back towards Sand Beach for a total walk of just under 1.5 miles.

5

Great Head and Gorham Mountain

GREAT HEAD (EASY)

This short, moderately easy hike provides excellent views of the island's rocky coast and out to the horizon line on the Atlantic.

Although the 2.0-mile loop can be done by fording the small stream on the east end of Sand Beach, the best place to start is at the paved parking area on the dead-end park road that heads south from the Schooner Head Overlook intersection.

Hit the trail and take your first obvious left. The path, which is quite wide although rocky, descends gradually toward the shore. Numerous social (unofficial) trails cut down to the massive granite ledges with their fine views and numerous tide pools. Stay to the left as you continue your trip through an intersection and up to the high point of the 145-foot-tall Great Head itself. The rubble of a stone tower, once used as a tea house, is evident at the top.

MAP 5: GREAT HEAD & GORHAM MTN.

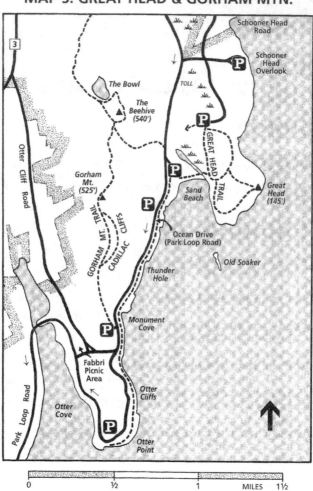

Schooner Head Road

Schooner Head Overlook

The Bowl

The Beehive (540')

TOLL

3

Otter Cliff Road

Gorham Mt. (525')

GORHAM MT. TRAIL

CADILLAC CLIFFS

GREAT HEAD TRAIL

Sand Beach

Great Head (145')

Ocean Drive (Park Loop Road)

Old Soaker

Thunder Hole

Monument Cove

Fabbri Picnic Area

Otter Cliffs

Otter Cove

Park Loop Road

Otter Point

0   ½   1   MILES   1½

Continue west along the peninsula. Fabulous views of Ocean Drive, Newport Cove, and the ledge "Old Soaker" will unfold. Do not try to descend to the many ocean caves along the cliff face. Several people, including well-trained and equipped technical climbers, have died in the attempt.

The most unusual geologic feature on this walk is Sand Beach. More than just sand, much of the beach is made up from billions of crushed bits of shells. During summer, swimmers enjoy the brisk 54-degree waters.

In 1911 the schooner *Tay* ran aground on Sand Beach, scattering its cargo of lumber. When winter waves carve the dunes at the back of the beach, the ribs of the vessel sometimes protrude.

Head north on the trail, which now traverses the remains of an old road, to return to the parking area or take a right at the trail intersection just south of the Sand Beach turnoff to cut back east across the head through a grove of young white birches. All vegetation on Great Head is still recovering from the aftereffects of the Great Fire of '47, which blew itself out in a great, wind-whipped fireball that leapt from the head and extinguished itself out over the ocean.

GORHAM MOUNTAIN (MODERATE)

A hike up 525-foot-tall Gorham Mountain along the Ocean Drive in Acadia National Park traverses some of the most interesting and diverse terrain the island has to offer.

The walk begins at the Gorham Mountain Parking Area on the right about 0.25 mile past Thunder Hole. The trail leaves the northwest corner of the lot and passes over ledges as it begins a gradual ascent. In spring and after heavy rains this trail can be very wet.

About 0.3 mile from the start, an intersection is reached. On the south face of a massive boulder here is a bronze plague dedicated to "Waldron Bates, Pathfinder." Bates, a Philadelphia lawyer, was instrumental in the layout and design of numerous trails on the island's eastern side. His innovative cairn design of a flat rock across two pedestals with an indicator stone on top is being restored to historic trails on the east side of MDI. Although the trail splits here, it will rejoin later on. Take the Cadillac Cliffs Trail to the right and descend slightly before traversing along the base of the cliffs that make up the mountain's southern flank. This path has you going over and even under massive boulders. In several places it is easy to see from the way in which the rocks are worn that the cliffs were once the shoreline when sea levels were higher.

After about 0.5 mile, the trail rejoins the main path, which sticks to the ridgeline. Several more steep ascents are needed before breaking out onto the wide-open summit plain at just under a mile. Views are spectacular from Sand Beach to the east to Otter Cliffs to the west. To the north, Cadillac, Dorr, and Champlain Mountains loom. Leave time to tarry at the summit.

Return using the ridgeline option to the parking lot. Or continue north, dropping, steeply at times, into the valley between Gorham and Halfway Mountains. Turn right on the Bowl Trail, which will take you back to Ocean Drive. Head right again and take the shore walk, which parallels Ocean Drive, back to your parking area, for a total hike of 2.5 miles.

6

Day Mountain and Hunter's Beach

DAY MOUNTAIN (MODERATE)

Day Mountain is another of Acadia's lesser peaks that offers rewards far beyond its 580-foot summit.

The trail starts in Seal Harbor, across from the parking area on Route 3, about 1.5 miles west of Blackwoods Campground. Just down the road is a monument to Samuel de Champlain, who named Mount Desert Island in 1604. The land around the monument was the first parcel given to a preserve that eventually became Acadia National Park.

The trail rises gently through open woods and crosses a carriage path a little over 0.25 mile from its start.

The way becomes more steep but still moderate for another 0.25 mile before again crossing a carriage road. Here, walkers have a choice. They can continue on the trail to the summit, crossing the meandering summit carriage road once more, or they can take the carriage road the rest of the way. Many

MAP 6: DAY MTN. & HUNTER'S BEACH

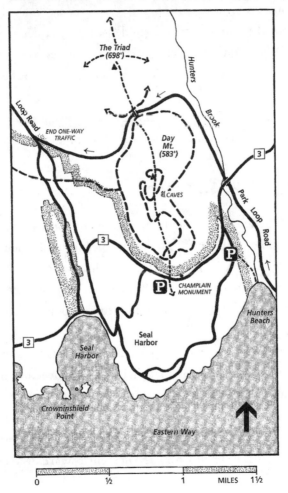

like the carriage road route as it offers better views in more directions.

From the summit, where guided carriage rides from the nearby Wildwood Stable let you savor the sunset, views extend 360 degrees. A foot trail to the north leads down to the stable complex.

Retrace your steps, or vary the route using the carriage road, to return to your car, for a total trip of about 2.0 miles.

HUNTER'S BEACH (EASY)

Hunter's Beach is one of the quintessential spots on Mount Desert Island that typify the natural beauty and splendor of this place. To reach the parking area, head west on Route 3 and take the first left about 0.8 mile past the entrance to the Blackwoods Campground. The trailhead is about 0.2 mile farther on the left.

There is only enough room for five or six cars here and that is as it should be. If Hunter's Beach becomes overrun, no one will be able to enjoy its magic. If the lot is full please consider coming back later or trying another day.

The trail begins on level ground behind the parking area and then quickly begins an easy descent towards the cobble beach. After a short distance, an elaborate footbridge, built by volunteer trail crews, is crossed. The trail then drops more over tree roots. On the left, Hunter's Brook can be heard first, then seen. The trail follows the brook a short ways, crossing a side channel on boulders. Listen now for the roar of the waves and see if you can smell the salt spray. The final 200-foot section passes through thick trees that frame a magnificent view of the offshore waters that unfolds as you emerge from the forest.

Hunter's Beach itself is a typical steep cobble beach composed of hundreds of thousands of stones rounded and worn smooth by the sea. It is barely 100 yards long wedged between high cliffs. The beach is reformed with each storm. If the waves are large enough you can hear the stones tumbling and grinding over themselves as the waters churns them over and over. Crushed lobster traps and worn driftwood above the high tide seaweed line testify to the ocean's power.

Often, Hunter's Brook disappears into the rocks only to emerge lower on the shore.

At low tide, be sure to explore the steep chasm to the east. Notice how the ocean exploits the weakness of one kind of rock while the granite remains strong. Smooth ledges here make a great picnic spot.

MAP 7: PEMETIC MOUNTAIN

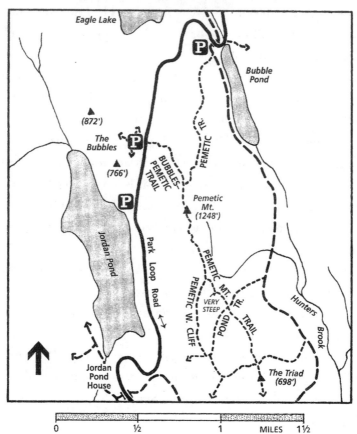

Eagle Lake

Bubble Pond

(872')

The Bubbles

(766')

Pemetic Mt. (1248')

Jordan Pond

PEMETIC TR.

BUBBLES-PEMETIC TRAIL

Park Loop Road

PEMETIC MT.

PEMETIC TR.

PEMETIC W. CLIFF

VERY STEEP

POND TRAIL

Hunters Brook

Jordan Pond House

The Triad (698')

| 0 | ½ | 1 | MILES 1½ |

7

Pemetic Mountain

PEMETIC MOUNTAIN LOOP (STRENUOUS)

Despite its major status with a summit of 1248 feet, Pemetic Mountain does not experience the same heavy use as other mountains.

Only one loop hike is possible without more than a mile of hoofing it on a busy paved road.

The most popular route up Pemetic begins in the Bubble Pond Parking Area along the Park Loop Road. Here, years ago, park officials actually uprooted a paved parking lot on the lake shore and replaced it with paradise in the form of new trees and shrubs. Take the carriage road south. The trail heads off to the right in .1 mile.

Starting gradually, the Pemetic Trail steadily gets steeper as it climbs through open spruce woods. After 0.5 mile it levels off some and the first views to the east open up as the path follows the top of steep cliffs. After turning away from the east slope, the incline moderates. The Bubbles Pemetic Trail enters from the right. The top is reached after a total walk of 1.25 miles. The

63

summit consists of several independent granite knobs and there are good views in all directions.

To make a long loop, head south down the Pemetic South Ridge Trail. You will pass several interesting small marshes nestled in bowls carved out of the mountain's granite.

At the intersection in 0.5 mile, the Pemetic East Cliff Trail to the left offers a shortcut but is extremely steep and wet in places. Continue straight for another 0.5 mile to the Bubble and Jordan Pond Path in the valley between Pemetic and the Triad. Turn left and after short climb, descend gradually on a relatively smooth path for .6 mile to a carriage road. Left on the carriage road will take you back 1.5 miles to the start, for a total distance of just under 4.5 miles.

BUBBLES PEMETIC (STRENUOUS)

Another possible up-and-back route to Pemetic's summit is the Bubble Pemetic Trail. This 0.5-mile trail rises steeply from the Bubble Rock Parking Area on the Park Loop Road. About half-way up, the trail enters a narrow canyon cut by a seasonal stream. At its deepest it is 15 feet deep. A wooden ladder at the head allows curious hikers to escape. Those who prefer can take the alternate route along the lip of the chasm to the south. It connects with the Pemetic Trail about 0.2 mile north of the summit.

West of Jordan Pond

SARGENT MOUNTAIN (STRENUOUS)

Farthest removed from any paved roads, and with only foot access, the 1373-foot summit of Sargent Mountain is the wildest and most alpine-like of any in the park. Its broad, open, windswept plain, shrubby vegetation, and lichen-encrusted rock make this peak more kin to those above treeline in the White Mountains or Baxter State Park.

The best walk up Sargent Mountain begins at the Parkman Mountain Parking Area on the east side of Route 198 where it crests on its way into Northeast Harbor. Follow the path out of the parking area and turn right on the carriage road, then left after a short distance. Stay on the winding carriage road for just under a mile. Stop at the second of two graceful granite arch bridges and turn left on the Hadlock Brook Trail.

In spring, or after moderate rainfall, the waterfall on

MAP 8: WEST OF JORDAN POND

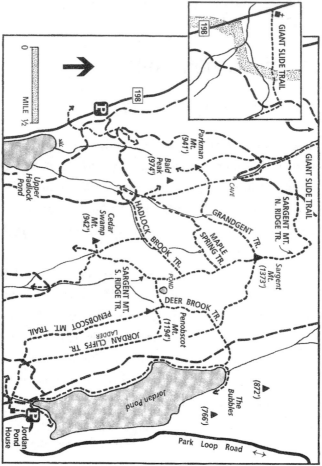

Hadlock Brook, the tallest on Mount Desert Island, should be in full force as clear waters splash down the 30-foot drop.

From here, the trail crisscrosses the brook on a moderate grade. After crossing the brook for the last time, the trail begins to climb very steeply until it reaches some open granite ledges that provide good views to the west. A short section of trail through shrubby trees and one last steep incline over bare rock and you are up on the open ridgeline. Turn left for the just over 0.5-mile stroll to the summit over vast blueberry barrens and bare rock. Late in the summer, striking red/orange wood lilies, which are found in only a very few exposed mountain and coastal locations, are in bloom.

Tufted grass and dark mysterious rain pools give Sargent an almost tundra-like feel. Heavy winds are not uncommon from any direction. Total distance to the top is approximately 2.0 miles.

At one time a wooden fire tower was located at the summit, but only a massive cairn of weathered rocks remains. Rusting wire and an occasional iron bar in the ledge are the only evidence of past structures.

To return, backtrack to the last major intersection and turn right toward Maple Spring. Located at a low spot on the mountainside, this spring has water most of the year. The trail rises for a short distance over one of Sargent's arms before dropping steeply through thick forest on a series of switchbacks.

After 0.5 mile, the trail turns sharply south and descends into the valley created by one branch of Hadlock Brook. The trail follows the tumbling and cascading brook back to the first carriage road bridge you crossed. Turn right here and return to the car by carriage road. Total trip distance about 4.0 miles.

GIANT SLIDE TRAIL (STRENUOUS)

One of the more interesting ways up Sargent Mountain is by the Giant Slide Trail, which begins along Route 198 on the way toward Northeast Harbor. Vehicles can be parked along the road. Note: It no longer uses part of a private road near an old stone church.

The trail rises gradually, heading east through verdant forests, occasionally crossing wet areas on bog walks. Just before intersecting the carriage road, the path passes through some nice groves of mature trees.

After crossing the carriage road the trail turns south and begins to rise more steeply. It follows Sargent Brook with its many small waterfalls. In clefts where the sun never reaches it is not unusual to find ice remaining even in late May. About

0.5 mile from the carriage road is an intersection. A right goes up and over another carriage road toward Parkman Mountain. A left heads up Sargent Mountain's North Ridge Trail to the summit at 2.1 miles. Stay straight and the trail soon levels off and crosses a second carriage road. Just ahead is the Giant Slide, a cave created when a massive slab of granite calved off a nearby cliff and slid into the brook. The trail goes through the 25-foot-long cave on step stones. It is impassable in high water.

Soon another intersection is reached. Left heads up the Grandgent Trail to the summit, for a total distance of 2.25 miles. The trail on the right rises steeply 0.2 mile to the top of Parkman Mountain, with its own impressive views. Straight brings you through a narrow valley where a central spring creates streams that flow north and south. This trail descends steeply to a carriage road on the south side of Parkman Mountain.

PENOBSCOT MOUNTAIN (STRENUOUS)

Penobscot Mountain offers fine views and a wide, barren ridge and summit. At 1194 feet, it is the fifth highest on the island.

Begin in the Jordan Pond House overflow parking area located at the south end of the pond just off the Park Loop

Road. Take the path to the Pond House itself, past the gift shop to the trail that leads west down a short hill to the carriage road. The Spring Trail begins on a footbridge just across the carriage road and slightly to the right.

The path begins to rise immediately with several steeper sections. A set of stone steps leads to the next carriage road crossing in 0.5 mile. The Penobscot Mountain Trail begins straight across on steep ledges that may require the use of hands.

The trail switchbacks up the east side of the mountain, occasionally using wooden handrails and plank bridges. At one point the trail, about five feet wide, has a smooth cliff 20 feet high on the left and a drop of 30 to 40 feet on the right. Rough footing makes ankle injuries common. In several spots, hikers must use hands to help boost themselves up narrow clefts.

After about another 0.25 mile the trail levels out. Where it emerges from the woods there are smooth ledges and wonderful views to the east.

In a short distance the trail turns sharp right and begins the ascent over open ledge. The trail to the left is the continuation of the Penobscot Mountain Trail and ends at a carriage road to the south. Several major plateaus, which turn out to be false summits, are encountered on the way to the summit. Finally, in just over 1.5 mile, the summit is reached. Again, there are great views in all directions.

From the summit head north down a steep, and sometimes slippery, incline to the col between Sargent and Penobscot. Stay straight at the intersection and walk the easy 0.1 mile to Sargent Mountain Pond, a cool, welcome respite on hot days. Once called Lake of the Clouds and also known as the Frog Pond, it is a great place for a quick dip or to stop for lunch. Trail crews have built several log benches at this site. Geologists claim it is "Maine's first lake" because it would have been the first fresh-water body created when glaciers receded 10,000 years ago.

After a swim, head back to the intersection and turn left to head down the Deer Brook Trail. Descend quickly and pass unmarked Cedar Spring. About 0.5 mile from the intersection another intersection is reached.

SARGENT EAST CLIFFS TRAIL (STRENUOUS)
JORDAN CLIFFS TRAIL (LADDER)

At this intersection the Sargent East Cliffs Trail on the left (north) ascends steeply in places, 0.8 mile to the summit of Sargent Mountain.

To the right (south) is the Jordan Cliffs Trail, which skirts along Penobscot Mountain's east face and is very steep and rugged. There are several sections with ladder rungs and hand railings, as well as exposed narrow ledges that are angled and very slippery when wet.

Many hikers prefer to hike this trail from the south, where it begins on a carriage road above Jordan Pond House.

The Deer Brook Trail continues to descend along the brook. Just before coming out on a carriage road, you must negotiate a massive tangle of tree roots. These roots beneath your feet are stars, however. They were featured in a scene in the Stephen King horror movie *Pet Sematary*.

Once at the carriage road, look to the left to check out another unique granite bridge. Then head left (south) back toward the Jordan Pond House on the carriage road for a hike of just under four miles.

Another option is to take the trail that continues to descend at the bridge to the shore of Jordan Pond. Turn right and follow the Jordan Pond Trail (see related description) along the water's edge back to the start.

9

Around Jordan Pond

(MODERATE)

At just over three miles, the walk around Jordan Pond can't be considered short, although because it sports few changes in elevation it is considered moderately easy. The pond is a reservoir and swimming or wading is not allowed.

The path, which skirts the lake for its entire journey, is not especially difficult to negotiate, although there is some rough footing in the "tumbledown" area at the pond's northwest end. A narrow log "bogwalk" runs for 0.8 of a mile on the west side of the pond. Because it is elevated several feet off the ground and is as narrow as 8 inches in places, excellent balance and agility are required.

Begin your walk in the boat ramp parking area located at the south end of the pond just off the Park Loop Road. Take the short nature trail that cuts down to the pond or walk to the bottom of the boat ramp road and turn right. Stop, though and enjoy one of the most impressive vistas in the park.

MAP 9: AROUND JORDAN POND

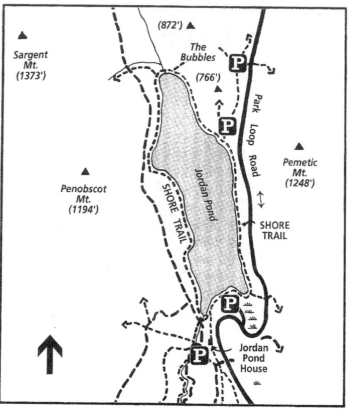

Sargent Mt. (1373')

(872') ▲

The Bubbles

(766')

Park Loop Road

Pemetic Mt. (1248')

Penobscot Mt. (1194')

Jordan Pond

SHORE TRAIL

SHORE TRAIL

Jordan Pond House

0   ½   1   MILES   1½

At the north end of the pond are the Bubbles, reportedly an adaptation of the name "bubbies." Legend also holds they were named by a summer gentleman who said the distinctive mounds reminded him of his rather well-endowed girlfriend named Bubbles.

The path runs smooth for a 0.25 mile and crosses a marshy cove on a causeway of large flat stones. A side trail here turns east and connects with the Park Loop Road. The smooth, wide trail heads north for nearly a mile to an intersection with the trail from the Bubbles Parking Area. This is another possible start and end point for the loop.

As the trail skirts the base of the South Bubble, check the cliffs above for technical climbers. At the north end of the pond the trail passes an intersection with the trail that ascends steeply between the Bubbles. It then crosses a stream on a unique "A" frame truss bridge made of logs. After an intersection with a trail that heads north and west and connects with a carriage road higher up the mountain, the path heads back down the western side of the lake, over the tumbledown and along the bog walk.

If you are tired of walking along the lake, take the trail to the carriage road. It rises very steeply and ends near a magnificent arch bridge. Both the trail and the carriage path will lead you back toward the pond house.

After crossing the Jordan Pond outlet stream, head east again to the launch ramp and your car.

If you time things right, stop at the Jordan Pond House for their famous tea and popovers on the lawn. It is an island tradition going back nearly 100 years. Hiking attire is just fine.

10

The Bubbles and Connors Nubble

NORTH AND SOUTH BUBBLES (MODERATE)

The top of South Bubble (766 feet) is one of the most popular climbs in the park and only moderately strenuous. In the past few years trail crews have rebuilt sections to reduce erosion and make footing easier. The result is a heavily engineered trail that gets the job done.

The most direct route begins at the Bubble Parking Area on the Park Loop Road. The trail leaves the west side of the lot and heads west. Turn right after 100 yards. Pass an intersection with the trail down to Jordan Pond. Stay on the Bubble Mountain Trail as it curves gradually to the west on an old logging road. After a short distance, the trail turns hard left and due west as it rises very steeply on log and stone steps to the swale between the twin peaks. A right turn part way up at a major intersection will take you up a very steep and rugged trail to the top of the somewhat higher (872 feet) North Bubble.

MAP 10: THE BUBBLES & CONNERS NUBBLE

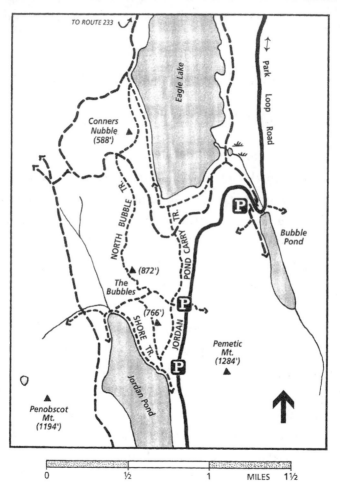

TO ROUTE 233

Eagle Lake

Park Loop Road

Conners Nubble (588')

NORTH BUBBLE TR.

POND CARRY TR.

P

Bubble Pond

(872')

The Bubbles

(766')

SHORE TR.

JORDAN

P

Pemetic Mt. (1284')

P

Jordan Pond

Penobscot Mt. (1194')

| 0 | ½ | 1 | MILES | 1½ |

Stay straight, however, to go to South Bubble and in less than 0.5 mile from the start go left at the intersection over more gradual inclines for another 0.25 mile to the top. Along the way take the marked side trail to visit Bubble Rock. Stay on marked trails to reduce environmental degradation. The size of a small house, this boulder is a glacial erratic left atop the Bubble when an ice sheet a mile thick treated more than 10,000 years ago.

Originally Mount Desert Island was one large ridge running in an east-west direction. As the glacier pushed at it from the north, it finally cut through, leaving the north-south ridges seen today. Lakes filled the deep cuts between the hills. As the ice moved southward it created smooth inclines on the north sides of hills as it rode up and over. As it headed down the other side it tore off large blocks of rock, leaving the cliffs evident today. According to Geologist Carleton Chapman, Bubble Rock was torn from another mountain more than 20 miles to the northwest.

Back on the trail, pass the summit at just over 0.5 mile from the start and continue down slightly to the ledges overlooking Jordan Pond to the south. The cliffs below are popular with technical climbers.

To vary your route back, turn left at the intersection in the swale and drop steeply over loose boulders to the north end of Jordan Pond. Go left again for 0.5 mile to the Jordan Pond Carry Trail intersection, turn left again for about 0.5 mile until it is time to turn right for the 100-yard path to the parking area.

CONNORS NUBBLE (MODERATE)

Standing on the top of Conners Nubble, overlooking Eagle Lake and dwarfed by the massive mountains to the east and west, you cannot help feeling like the conductor of some antediluvian orchestra embraced by the instruments of earth's majesty.

Start by parking on the north end of Eagle Lake on Route 233 and head sound on the carriage road that follows the west side of the lake. About 1.5 miles from the start take the trail that heads off to the left and crosses a wet area. Turn right at the next intersection (a left turn leads along the shore of the lake over a very rough track). The trail up Connors begins with gradual ascent through open woods on the north slope. Just before hitting the flat, open summit, about 2 miles from the start, the trail gets very steep as it climbs the east side of the knob.

The open, step-like nature of the 588-foot summit provides endless nooks where you can escape the constant wind. Eagle Lake shimmers below to the east, while the glint of reflected light from vehicles climbing to the top of Cadillac Mountain can be seen. To the south, Pemetic Mountain and the North Bubble are almost close enough to touch. Sargent and Penobscot Mountains tower to the west.

Retrace your steps or take the short, and somewhat steep, trail that continues south from the summit a short ways to a carriage road. Turn right and stay right at the next intersection to return to the north end of the lake. Total distance is around 4.0 miles for out and retrace and 5.0 miles for the alternate route.

MAP 11: NORUMBEGA MTN.

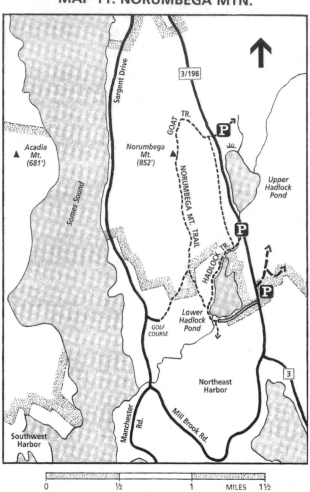

11

Norumbega Mountain

(STRENUOUS)

When French explorer Samuel de Champlain first sighted Mount Desert Island in 1604 he was on a mission of discovery. His goal was the fabled golden-walled city of Norumbega, which native tribesmen claimed existed somewhere in the vicinity of present-day Bangor.

Champlain was not the only one who was bitten by the legend, and naming the mountain that looms on the eastern side of Somes Sound Norumbega recognizes the legend's place in history.

Most hikes up Norumbega begin at the parking area above Upper Hadlock Pond along Route 198. The Goat Trail, aptly named due to its steep ascent, begins here and climbs quickly up the mountain's eastern flank. After 0.25 mile the trail takes a more gradual incline on the way to the 852-foot summit at 0.5 mile. In season, blueberries provide a refreshing trailside treat.

While views from the summit are grand, Norumbega is not broad and open like most of the island's larger peaks.

The trail continues south, passing through attractive, open coniferous forest, descending gradually toward the south end of Lower Hadlock Pond. (Water supply, no swimming or wading.)

At the trail intersection, a right turn will take you a short ways to the Northeast Harbor Golf Course. Straight leads a short ways to a parking area near the dam. A left turn on the trail that leads along the west shore of the pond is worth the trip and allows you to return to your start with only minimal elevation gain for a total trip of about 2.5 miles.

Ironically, over the years, Bangor went on to become the Queen City and hub of lumbering in Maine. For many who made their fortune there it had indeed become a "city of gold."

12

Parkman and Cedar Swamp Mountains

PARKMAN MOUNTAIN, BALD PEAK (MODERATE)

Parkman Mountain at 941 feet in height and sister summit Bald Peak, 974 feet, are often bypassed by those on the way to higher summits to the east. But that is their loss.

Begin at the Parkman Mountain Parking Area on the east side of Route 198 where it crests on the way into Northeast Harbor. Follow the wide path out of the parking area and turn right on the carriage road, then left after a short distance. Stay on the winding carriage road for less than a quarter mile until you see the Parkman Mountain trail post on the left. Ascend gradually, cross another carriage road after a few yards, and then plunge into the quiet forest. The trail zig-zags up an unnamed ridge with occasional views. Some sections are steep with slick footing and may require use of hands, although drop-offs are not percipitous.

MAP 12: PARKMAN & CEDAR SWAMP MTNS.

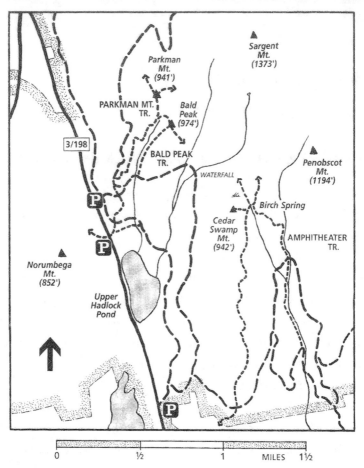

In 0.75 mile you enter the col between Parkman and Bald Peak. A left takes you quickly to the summit of Parkman, a right to Bald Peak.

Parkman offers splendid views of sheltered Somesville, site of the first permanent village on Mount Desert Island in 1761, then called "Betwixt the Hills," to the northwest.

Bald Peak, at 947 feet, has good views of Upper Hadlock Pond immediately below and Northeast Harbor and the offshore Cranberry Isles beyond. Both peaks also offer good vantage to see the larger mountains to the west, including Norumbega.

A trail descending on the south side of Bald Peak allows hikers to avoid backtracking. It reaches a carriage road after 0.4 mile. Head right and later take the carriage road that bears left ahead to return to your car for a 2.0-mile hike.

CEDAR SWAMP MOUNTAIN (MODERATE)

With one of the gentlest gradients of any summit on Mount Desert Island, Cedar Swamp Mountain is a very enjoyable, albeit long, walk of almost 4.0 miles. Avoiding backtracking, however, involves a bit more scrambling.

Begin at the Brown Mountain Gatehouse on Route 198 just above Northeast Harbor. Take the carriage road to the right and then go right again at the intersection, and continue to where the trail crossed the carriage road about 0.75 mile from the start.

Turn left onto the trail and begin a gradual ascent over ledges and through a fragrant forest. After about 0.5 mile, views begin to open up to the east and west. Farther along, open ledges and areas of low, shrubby vegetation make views even better. Just before reaching the top, the trail skirts cliffs on the east overlooking a high-sided valley known as the Amphitheater.

When you reach the highest ground, a side trail leads several yards to the actual summit (942 feet), about 1.75 miles from the start.

The main trail descends steeply through medium-size boulders to a narrow valley between Cedar Swamp Mountain and Penobscot Mountain. Just down a ways from the four-way trail intersection is Birch Spring, which has reliable water for most of the year. The cedar swamp for which the mountain is named is actually located farther north in this narrow valley. It is unusual to find such a wet, grassy area atop a mountain and it is worth a quick side trip.

Take a right at the spring and head down steeply on the Amphitheater Trail, which features several open ledges. Turn right again when you hit the carriage road to head back to the start. Tarry a while at the impressive granite arch bridge on the carriage road. The total distance is around 4.0 miles.

West of Somes Sound

ACADIA MOUNTAIN (MODERATE)

Overlooking the west shore of Somes Sound, Acadia Mountain is one of the most popular in the park. The 0.5-mile trail to the second and lower summit has several steep sections but is easy enough to be included on the list of guided walks offered by the National Park Service. The toughest section is the 0.25 mile descent from the ridge south to the end of the Man O' War Brook Fire Road. It can be avoided by simply retracing your steps.

Park on the west side of Route 102 in the well-marked Acadia Mountain Parking Area. The trail begins right across the road. It heads north a short ways before crossing the fire road and turning to the northeast. It rises steadily with several steep sections before mounting the relatively flat summit punctuated by gnarly jack pines. At the 681-foot summit, and again at a lower part of the ridge to the east, views are excellent.

MAP 13: WEST OF SOMES SOUND

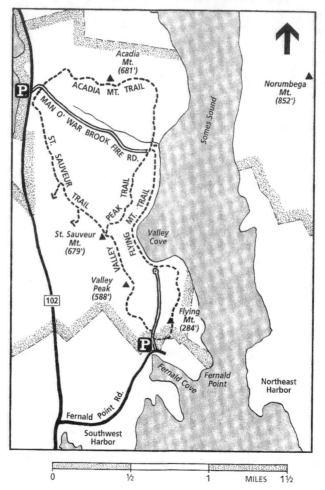

0 ½ 1 MILES 1½

To avoid backtracking, descend down a very steep trail to the fire road. Be sure to take a short side trip left to see where the brook empties into the sound. The brook got its name from the Revolutionary-era warships that would use the waterfall that tumbles into the sea at the end of the brook to fill their water casks.

Turn right on the fire road for a long yet steady uphill back to Route 102, for a total trip of just under 2.0 miles.

During the hotter months, be sure to bring your swimsuit. A trail leads downhill from the parking area on Route 102 to a popular swimming ledge on Echo Lake. No life guards are on duty as the ledges are not an official Park Service beach.

ST. SAUVEUR MOUNTAIN (MODERATE)

Those wishing to hike up 679-foot St. Sauveur Mountain have several options. The most gradual ascent begins at the Acadia Mountain Parking Area on Route 102. Cross the road and take the trail that heads right and rises gradually toward the summit. Numerous open ledges and stands of jack pines will be encountered. While not as flat and open as some on the island, the summit, reached in a mile, has splendid views in all directions. Take the trail that heads north and descends steeply into the

Man o' War Brook valley. Notice how the vegetation and terrain change on this darker and damper side of the mountain. Turn left on the fire road to return (see Acadia Mountain directions). This route covers 2.25 miles.

Another option is to continue southeast from the summit (there are two trails to pick from), descending to Valley Peak. The trails merge and descend sharply to the Valley Cove Road, for a total distance from the summit of .75 mile. Turn left and stroll down the road to a pretty cove surrounded by impressive cliffs. A trail heads west and then north along the cove and connects up with the fire road along Man o' War Brook. Turn left to return to the parking area, for a total trip of 3.75 miles.

FLYING MOUNTAIN (MODERATE)

You can't honestly say you've climbed them all on Mount Desert Island until you have topped the often overlooked Flying Mountain near Southwest Harbor.

Turn off Route 102 onto the Fernald Point Road where you see a sign for the Causeway Club Golf Course. About a mile down the road, at the end of Fernald Cove, park at the gated dirt road on the left. The trail starts right up, rising steeply to the treed yet open summit in less than 0.5 mile.

At only 284 feet above sea level, Flying Mountain is no Everest. But it offers stunning views up Somes Sound, considered the only true fjord in eastern North America. Due east, across the sound, is Northeast Harbor. To the south lies the great harbor of Mount Desert. Immediately below on Fernald Point is the site of the first attempted settlement on Mount Desert Island. A party of forty or so French Jesuits, under the direction of Father Pierre Baird, settled there in 1613. Their excitement at finding such a sheltered place was short-lived. About a month after arrival, an English warship, tipped off by Indians, attacked the colony and sent the occupants packing.

Retrace your steps to return or continue north on the Valley Cove Trail that leads down a small talus slope to the end of the Valley Peak Road on the shore of the cove. Head left to return to the parking area, for a total length of approximately 1.0 mile.

MAP 14: SHIP HARBOR & WONDERLAND

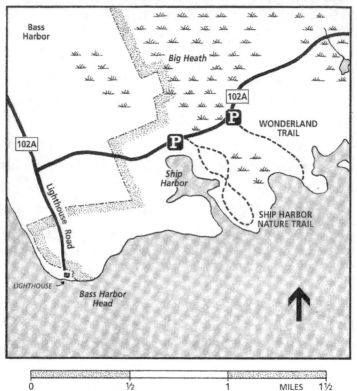

14

Ship Harbor and Wonderland

SHIP HARBOR NATURE TRAIL (EASY)

The Ship Harbor Trail is an easy and fun walk for the entire family and an ideal first trip to acquaint visitors to some of the ecology of Mount Desert Island. Booklets to help explain stops along the self-guided trail are available at the trailhead.

According to famed historian Samuel Eliot Morison, the harbor got its name after a local vessel, pursued by an English man o' war, sought refuge in the inlet and ran aground during the Revolution.

Starting from the well-marked parking area along Route 102A, the trail is an elongated figure eight. Direction of travel is merely a matter of personal preference. Signs help to explain environmental processes and identify trees and lichens.

As the trail reaches the ocean, look to the east to spot Long Ledge, which was the scene of a tragic mystery in the winter of 1739–40. The sailing vessel *Grand Design* approached Ship

Harbor mistaking it for the mouth of a river. It struck the ledge and sank. Between the cold and minimal provisions, there were few survivors. They were rescued months after subsisting on clams and blueberries. Immediately after the wreck, some of the settlers and crew had set out for the settlement at Warren, more than 100 miles to the west. They were never heard from again.

The 1.3-mile Ship Harbor Trail is an easy walk with a few medium upgrades and is an excellent place to spend an afternoon discovering some of the secrets of Acadia's forests and shores.

WONDERLAND (EASY)

Slightly closer to the Seawall Campground on Route 102A is the parking area and trailhead for the Wonderland Trail. This 0.5-mile point-to-point walk is about a mile round trip on a wide, mostly level path. It features modest elevation gain as it tops a 60-foot hill midway through your journey. The walk begins in mixed woods and ends in a grove of spruce along the shore overlooking the ocean and a peninsula with a pretty pebble beach, tide pools, and granite ledges.

15

Beech Mountain and Canada Cliffs

BEECH MOUNTAIN (STRENUOUS)

With its distinctive fire tower, Beech Mountain, at 839 feet, is a popular hiking destination. The fire tower, which is sometimes staffed by interpretive personnel in summer, is closed and only used for fire spotting during extremely dangerous fire conditions.

Most visitors park in the Beech Mountain lot, nestled between the east and west peaks. It is only a short walk west to the summit on the Beech Mountain Trail. It is only 0.5 mile of steady ascent, with hikers deciding which of two branches to actually use to reach the top. The right-hand option offers the best views of Long Pond and the sunset.

Other trails that start on park fire roads near the end of Long Pond in Southwest Harbor offer pleasant walks through lush forests, although distances and elevation gain are greater. There is also a connector trail that loops back around to the

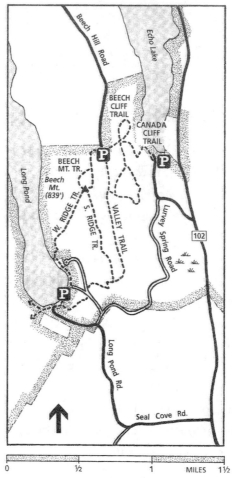

bottom of the Canada Cliffs Trail, starting at the south end of the cliffs on top. (See map.)

CANADA CLIFFS TRAIL (LADDER)

Beginning at the Echo Lake Beach Parking Area, the Canada Cliffs Trail is one of the most physically challenging on the island. Numerous wooden handrails, tall iron ladders, and the occasional handrail or iron railing are used to aid hikers in their ascent. This is not a trail for anyone who has a fear of heights.

The trail continues switchbacking up the cliffs before reaching the top of the eastern peak of Beech Mountain in 0.5 mile. There are several options for walking along the top of the cliffs. Hikers can do a short loop overlooking scenic Echo Lake or continue down a short steep grade to the parking area, where they can catch the Beech Mountain Trail to the fire tower.

MAP 16: WESTERN MTN. & SEAL COVE MARSH

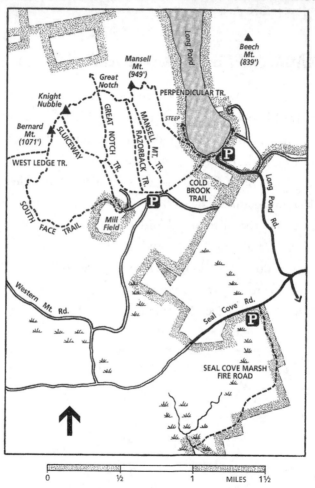

16

Western Mountain

Western Mountain is actually comprised of three distinct peaks, including Bernard Peak to the west, Knight Nubble in the center, and Mansell Mountain overlooking Long Pond to the east. Together, this trio offers a wonderful lengthy hike over three distinct wooded summits. Individually, each peak offers great opportunities for half-day trips.

BERNARD MOUNTAIN (STRENUOUS)

This trip begins at the gravel parking area off the Western Mountain Road. The South Face Trail rises gradually through thick forest on the remains of an old logging road, signs of which soon disappear. The first views to the west begin to appear after 0.52 mile. Short unmarked side trails lead to overlooks.

An intersection with the West Face Trail, which descends to Western Mountain Road, is reached after about a mile.

As the trail approaches the summit it passes through some

of the only old-growth forest remaining on Mount Desert Island. The open coniferous woods have an almost surreal appearance. The trail levels out for a short distance before reaching the 1071 foot summit, almost hidden in trees. A bit farther there is an open area with a log bench offering wonderful views to the north. The total trip is 1.8 miles.

To return, continue down a very steep descent into the col between Bernard and Knight Nubble. A right turn here on the Sluiceway Trail will return you past a small fire reservoir at the mountain's base to your vehicle.

KNIGHT NUBBLE (STRENUOUS)

To continue east across the Western Mountain Ridge, do not turn at the Sluiceway Trail and ascend steeply to the top of Knight Nubble. Just beyond the top there is a good ledge overlook to the southeast.

The trail continues to descend and then levels off through thick woods. One more major steep descent puts you at the bottom of the Great Notch. A right here will return you to the mountain's base on the Great Notch Trail.

A hiker's journal, kept in a box fastened to a tree, and log benches make the Great Notch an attractive place to pause.

The trail north from this intersection, the Western Mountain Trail, splits, with one branch ending on the Seal Cove Fire Road and the other curving out around Mansell Mountain to skirt the edge of Long Pond, becoming the Long Pond Trail.

MANSELL MOUNTAIN (STRENUOUS)

From the Great Notch, the trail heads east for the 949-foot summit of Mansell Mountain, passing over a series of distinct north-south humps. The terrain is a mix of open ledges and forest glens. Several steep trails leading right, down off the mountain, are passed, including the Razorback Trail and the Mansell Mountain Trail. After cutting north, the unremarkable summit is reached, for a total of 3.0 miles from the start.

Don't linger. Continue for another 0.25 mile to the wide-open ledges that overlook Long Pond. This is the best view Mansell has to offer.

To descend, take the Perpendicular Trail (Ladder). It starts by following a seasonal stream course and then running along the base of smooth granite cliffs. Several sections are very steep, with numerous stone steps. There are several iron rungs and one short ladder to negotiate.

Take a right when you reach the trail along the lake. Turn

right again just before reaching the pump house and stroll back to Mill Field along the gently undulating Cold Brook Trail as it passes through pretty woods. The total, full-length round trip is 4.75 miles.

BASS HARBOR MARSH FIRE ROAD (EASY)

Seldom visited by anyone, the smooth gravel Bass Harbor Marsh Fire Road makes for a pleasant afternoon's stroll (or short bike ride) through some of the wildest country in Acadia.

Park carefully off to the left (south) side of the Seal Cove Road, 0.4 mile west of the intersection with the Long Pond Road. The entrance to the fire road is overgrown, set back a ways, and not easy to spot. Be sure not to block the gate.

The road heads south, and then more westerly, climbing up and down over several low rises. Marshy cedar swamps alternate with pretty stretches of open woodland. Keep a careful eye out for the tracks and signs of white-tailed deer and coyotes, and, if you're lucky, evidence that one of the island's rare moose has passed that way.

After 1.5 miles the road ends at the backwater stream that leads to the tidal Bass Harbor Marsh. Reverse your route to return.

Appendix A

GPS COORDINATES OF ACADIA PEAKS

Acadia Mountain
· Latitude: 44.323413
· Longitude: -68.321961

Bald Peak
· Latitude: 44.33508
· Longitude: -68.283349

Beech Mountain
· Latitude: 44.310635
· Longitude: -68.345017

Bernard Peak
· Latitude: 44.302302
· Longitude: -68.371962

Cadillac Mountain
· Latitude: 44.352857
· Longitude: -68.223902

Cedar Swamp Mountain
· Latitude: 44.328413
· Longitude: -68.275849

Champlain Mountain
· Latitude: 44.350636
· Longitude: -68.193068

Connors Nubble
· Latitude: 44.355357
· Longitue: -68.255293

Day Mountain
· Latitude: 44.31008
· Longitude: -68.231681

Dorr Mountain
· Latitude: 44.354524
· Longitude: -68.215569

Flying Mountain
· Latitude: 44.303969
· Longitude: -68.313628

Gorham Mountain
· Latitude: 44.327302
· Longitude: -68.191679

Great Head
- Latitude: 44.328414
- Longitude: -68.174178

Huguenot Head
- Latitude: 44.353135
- Longitude: -68.199457

Kebo Mountain
- Latitude: 44.373413
- Longitude: -68.218347

Mansell Mountain
- Latitude: 44.306469
- Longitude: -68.361407

North Bubble
- Latitude: 44.344246
- Longitude: -68.256682

Norumbega Mountain
- Latitude: 44.324524
- Longitude: -68.296405

Parkman Mountain
- Latitude: 44.337857
- Longitude: -68.28446

Pemetic Mountain
- Latitude: 44.335913
- Longitude: -68.245292

Penobscot Mountain
- Latitude: 44.332858
- Longitude: -68.26668

Sargent Mountain
- Latitude: 44.34258
- Longitude: -68.272793

South Bubble
- Latitude: 44.338691
- Longitude: -68.254182

The Beehive
- Latitude: 44.333413
- Longitude: -68.188345

Appendix B

NAME ORIGINS

Acadia

Although many people long for the name Acadia to be connected with the story of Evangeline and the Acadian people made famous in Longfellow's epic poem, the similarity ends at the French root. Acadia comes from the term *L'Acadie*, the French version of an Indian word that means "the place." *La Cadie*, as it was sometimes written, refers to the entire original French claim to North America.

Mount Desert Island

Mount Desert Island was originally called *Pemetic* by the Native American Abnaki and means literally "range of tall mountains." Many mountains on MDI have Native American names.

The name Mount Desert Island is credited to French explorer Samuel de Champlain, who, upon viewing the island from the sea in September 1604, wrote in his log, "this island is very high and cleft into seven or eight mountains all in line. The summits of most of them are bare of trees, nothing but rock." Champlain named it *l'Isle des monts-déserts*—literally, Isle of Bare Mountains. Champlain was exploring the area under the auspices of French nobleman Sieur de Monts.

Down East

Most everyone knows "Down East" is in Maine and refers to the communities along the northeastern coast of Maine. But few understand why to go "Down" East you must go "up" the coast.

Although there are numerous explanations of the origin, the most satisfactory is that "Down East" is a seafaring term that had foundations in the fact that the prevailing wind is from the southwest. Therefore, sailboats going to Maine from the west and south sailed before the wind, an act described as "running downhill" because of the ease of sailing as compared to "beating up against it," going to windward.

Thus, a sailing vessel bound for Maine would "run" before the wind and go "downhill to the eastward," or, briefly, "Down East."

Appendix C

FOR MORE INFORMATION

Additional Reading

Abrell, Diana. *Pocket Guide to Carriage Roads of Acadia National Park 2nd Edition*. Camden, Maine, Down East Books, 2011.

Brechlin, Earl. *Bygone Bar Harbor*. Camden, Maine, Down East Books, 2002.

Kendall, David L. *Glaciers and Granite: A Guide to Maine's Landscape and Geology*. Unity, Maine, North Country Press, 1993.

Lenahan, Don. *The Memorials of Acadia National Park*. Bar Harbor, Maine, Published by the author, 2010.

Minutolo-Le, Audrey. *Pocket Guide to Biking on Mount Desert Island 2nd Edition,* Camden, Maine, Down East Books, 2012.

Newlin, William V.P.. *Guide to the Lakes and Ponds of Mt. Desert*. Camden, Down East Books, 1988.

O'Neil, Gladys, and G.W. Helfrich. *Lost Bar Harbor*. Camden, Maine, Down East Books, 1986.

Roberts, Ann Rockefeller. *Mr. Rockefeller's Roads*, Camden, Maine, Down East Books, 1990.

Web Sites

Local news/information: www.fenceviewer.com

Acadia National Park: www.nps.gov/acad

Friends of Acadia: www.friendsofacadia.org

Island Explorer: www.exploreacadia.com

Bar Harbor Chamber of Commerce: www.barharborinfo.org

Maine Weather: www.maine.gov/mema/weather/weather.htm